W9-AZG-398

Pronghorn

Long-Distance Runner!

by Natalie Lunis

Consultant: Jim Mason, Naturalist
Great Plains Nature Center
Wichita, Kansas
www.gpnc.org

BEARPORT
PUBLISHING

NEW YORK, NEW YORK

Credits

Cover, © Stephen J. Krasemann/All Canada Photos/Superstock; TOC, © PaulTessier/iStockphoto; 4–5, © Daniel Teetor/ Digital Outdoors Inc.; 6L, © Barbara Magnuson & Larry Kimball; 6R, © Werner Bollmann/Oxford Scientific/Photolibrary; 7, © Art Wolfe/Stone/Getty Images; 9, © Jeff Banke/Shutterstock; 10T, © Boris Z./Shutterstock; 10M, © Tim Fitzharris/Minden Pictures; 10B, © Tim Fitzharris/Minden Pictures; 11, © Donald M. Jones/Minden Pictures; 12, © franzfoto.com/Alamy; 13, © Charles G. Summers Jr./Wild Images; 14–15, © Peter Llewellyn; 16, © Tom & Pat Leeson; 17, © Winfried Wisniewski/age fotostock/SuperStock; 18, Courtesy of Prints Old & Rare; 19, © Leo Keeler/Alamy; 20–21, © J.L. "Woody" Wooden; 22, © Stephen J. Krasemann/All Canada Photos/Superstock; 23TL, © EcoPrint/Shutterstock; 23TR, © Anton Foltin/Shutterstock; 23BL, © kavram/Shutterstock; 23BM, © Donald M. Jones/Minden Pictures; 23BR, © franzfoto.com/Alamy.

Publisher: Kenn Goin
Editorial Director: Adam Siegel
Creative Director: Spencer Brinker
Original Design: Debrah Kaiser
Photo Researcher: Picture Perfect Professionals, LLC

Library of Congress Cataloging-in-Publication Data

Lunis, Natalie.
  Pronghorn : long-distance runner! / by Natalie Lunis.
     p. cm. — (Blink of an eye : superfast animals)
  Includes bibliographical references and index.
  ISBN-13: 978-1-936087-94-5 (library binding)
  ISBN-10: 1-936087-94-4 (library binding)
  1. Pronghorn—Juvenile literature. I. Title.
  QL737.U52L86 2011
  599.63'9—dc22

                              2010011127

For more information, write to Bearport Publishing Company, Inc., 101 Fifth Avenue, Suite 6R, New York, New York 10003. Printed in the United States of America in North Mankato, Minnesota.

072010
042110CGE

10 9 8 7 6 5 4 3 2 1

Contents

How Fast?. 4

Horns with Prongs. 6

Wide-Open Spaces 8

Nowhere to Hide 10

Flashing a Warning 12

Running Away 14

Long-Distance Champs 16

Almost Gone. 18

Forever Fast. 20

Built for Speed. 22

Glossary. 23

Index. 24

Read More. 24

Learn More Online. 24

About the Author 24

How Fast?

The pronghorn is the fastest-running animal in North America.

It can reach a top speed of 55 miles per hour (89 kph).

That's as fast as the speed limit on many highways.

The world's fastest human can run at a top speed of 23 miles per hour (37 kph). A racehorse can run at a top speed of 45 miles per hour (72 kph). A pronghorn can run faster than both.

Human
23 mph / 37 kph

Racehorse
45 mph / 72 kph

Pronghorn
55 mph / 89 kph

Horns with Prongs

Pronghorns get their name from the horns on their heads.

Only males have horns with branches, or **prongs**, however.

Females sometimes have horns, but their horns are smaller and plainer.

horn

prong

male pronghorn

horn

female pronghorn

7

Wide-Open Spaces

Most pronghorns live in the open, grassy areas of North America known as the **prairies**.

They eat the grasses and wildflowers that grow there.

Some pronghorns, however, live in desert areas.

They eat sagebrush, **cacti**, and other desert plants.

The prairies and deserts where pronghorns live are mostly in western North America.

Pronghorns in the Wild

Canada

United States

Mexico

Pacific Ocean

Atlantic Ocean

N
W E
S

■ Where pronghorns live

During the winter, pronghorns live in large groups called herds. During the rest of the year, they live in smaller groups.

9

Nowhere to Hide

In the wide-open spaces where pronghorns live, there is nowhere to hide from enemies.

The animals need to watch for coyotes, bobcats, wolves, and other animals that might attack them.

Luckily, pronghorns have sharp eyesight.

In fact, they can spot movement from three miles (5 km) away.

Also, because their eyes are high up on the sides of their heads, they can still see far even when their heads are down to eat grass.

coyote

bobcat

wolf

Pronghorns have an excellent sense of smell. So they can smell as well as see enemies from far away.

Flashing a Warning

As soon as a pronghorn spots danger, it lets out a loud snort.

The sound acts as a warning, letting other pronghorns know that there is trouble around.

Then the pronghorn sends out another warning signal—one that reaches herd members that are farther away.

The animal raises the hairs on the large white patch on its **rump** so that the patch grows bigger.

The signal looks almost like a flashing light.

It tells other pronghorns, "Run for your life!"

rump

flashing hairs

Pronghorns also release a skunk-like smell from their bodies when they sense danger. Like the snort and the flashing rump patch, the smell tells other pronghorns to run from danger.

13

Running Away

Warning signals sent by a pronghorn spread quickly through a herd.

Just as quickly, the animals take off.

They run together as a group.

Usually, a female leads the herd as they streak across the prairie or desert.

A male runs at the back, ready to fight off any enemy that is able to catch up.

Pronghorns usually form a line or an oval as they run from danger.

Long-Distance Champs

Pronghorns do not clock in as the fastest runners in the world.

That spot belongs to the cheetah— which has a top speed of 70 miles per hour (113 kph).

However, the cheetah can run that fast only for a few hundred yards (meters).

The pronghorn can keep running at about 30 miles per hour (48 kph) for several miles (kilometers).

In a long-distance race, it could easily outrun a cheetah.

Cheetahs live on the grasslands of Africa. They hunt antelopes that can run almost as fast as the pronghorn over long distances.

cheetah

antelope

17

Almost Gone

During the 1800s, pronghorns almost disappeared from the prairies.

Hunters shot millions of them as people settled the western parts of North America.

The settlers built farms and ranches on the grasslands and put up fences around them.

The pronghorns that were left had trouble surviving.

The herds were often cut off from the places where they had found water and safety during harsh weather.

HARPER'S WEEKLY.

JOURNAL OF CIVILIZATION.

Vol. XXXIII.—No. 1676.
NEW YORK, SATURDAY, FEBRUARY 2, 1889.
TEN CENTS A COPY.
WITH A SUPPLEMENT.

Before the mid-1800s, when settlers arrived in the West, there were around 35 million pronghorns living on the prairies. By the early 1900s, there were only about 20,000 left.

Forever Fast

During the early 1900s, the number of pronghorns started slowly going up.

People had stopped using the prairie lands for farms and ranches because they learned the earth there was too dry and rough.

Many people also started working to protect America's wild animals and the places where they lived.

Today, large herds of pronghorns once again roam the North American prairies.

With people's help, they will keep speeding along as the number one long-distance runner for a long time to come.

Today, there are about a million pronghorns living in North America. The largest herds are found in Wyoming and Montana.

Built for Speed

What makes a pronghorn such a fast runner? Here is how different parts of the animal's body help it reach its amazing speeds.

mouth is open when running to breathe in extra air

large heart and lungs send plenty of oxygen from the air that is breathed in to the muscles

a pad on the bottom of each hoof helps a pronghorn make a softer landing each time its foot touches the ground

legs are long, with strong bones and muscles

wide hooves grip the ground well at high speeds

Glossary

antelope (AN-tuh-lohp) a kind of hoofed animal that runs very fast

cacti (KAK-tye) plants that need little water to live and usually have sharp spikes

prairies (PRAIR-eez) large areas of flat land covered with grass

prongs (PRONGZ) the little branches on the horns of male pronghorns

rump (RUMP) the rear end of some animals, such as pronghorns

Index

antelopes 7, 17

cheetah 16–17

deserts 8, 14

enemies 10–11, 14

eyesight 10–11

females 6, 14

food 8, 10

herds 9, 12, 14, 18, 20–21

homes 8, 10, 18, 20–21

horns 6

hunters 18

males 6, 14

North America 8, 18, 20–21

prairies 8, 14, 18, 20

prongs 6

rump 12–13

sense of smell 11

settlers 18

speed 4–5, 16, 22

warning signals 12–13, 14

Read More

Doeden, Matt. *The World's Fastest Animals.* Mankato, MN: Capstone (2007).

Goldish, Meish. *Giraffes and Other Hoofed Mammals.* Chicago: World Book (2006).

Jackson, Tom. *Pronghorns.* Danbury, CT: Grolier (2008).

Learn More Online

To learn more about pronghorns, visit
www.bearportpublishing.com/BlinkofanEye

About the Author

Natalie Lunis has written many science and nature books for children. She lives in the Hudson River Valley, just north of New York City.